D0343232

PRINCESS POCAHONTAS
AND THE BLUE SPOTS

Princess Pocahontas and the Blue Spots

TWO PLAYS BY

Monique Mojica

women's
PRESS

CANADIAN CATALOGUING IN PUBLICATION DATA
Mojica, Monique, 1954-
    Princess Pocahontas and the blue spots
ISBN 0-88961-165-3

1. Indians of North America - Women - History - Drama.
2. Indians of North America - Women - Social conditions - Drama.
3. North America - Discovery and exploration - Drama. I. Title.

PS8576.055P7 1991   C812'.54   C91-095265-5
PR9199.3.M6P7 1991

"Princess Pocahontus and the Blue Spots" was originally published
in *Canadian Theatre Review* 64 (Fall 1990).

Cover illustration and design: Cheryl Henhawke
Photos: Jim Miller
Cover title, book design and typesetting: Sunday Harrison
Editing: Monique Mojica with Lenore Keeshig-Tobias
Copy editor: Claire Dineen

Published by Women's Press,
517 College St., #233, Toronto, Ontario M6G 4A2

This book was produced by the collective effort of Women's Press.
Women's Press gratefully acknowledges financial support from
the Canada Council and the Ontario Arts Council

Printed and bound in Canada. First printing, October 1991

    3 4 5   1998 1997 1996

PRINTED ON ACID-FREE PAPER

CONTENTS

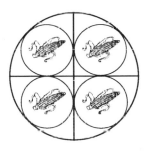

Princess Pocahontas
and the Blue Spots

Acknowledgements

My father, Mathis for always going back a few centuries to explain and for passing on his love of words.

My mother, Gloria for being so determined to get me to all those dance and drama classes.

Muriel Miguel for asking all the hard questions and for her visionary gift as a director.

Djanet Sears for being the ship's figurehead.

Alejandra Nuñez for a voice that causes a *terremoto* under my feet.

Shelly Teperman for the initial shove.

Maria Campbell for introducing me to Métis territory.

Marjorie Beaucage for research on the Métis women and for continuing to hold the mirror and a flame.

Billy Merasty for the Cree language connection.

Kate Lushington for her practical commitment to anti-racist work.

Ruth Dworin for her support, for teaching me to become computer literate, and for being a Jewish mother *extraodinaire*.

Dr. Hania Armengol for being such a dedicated healer.

The Native Canadian Centre of Toronto and the American Indian Community House of New York City for rehearsal space.

Native Earth Performing Arts

Nightwood Theatre

Theatre Passe Muraille

Jorge from "Los Incas" for research on Ima Sumac.

Fernando Hernández Perez for research on Malinche, his assistance during editing, and for standing with me in the Rainforest.

And my son, Bear: towards the next generation of healing.

Princess Pocahontas and the Blue Spots
is dedicated to Elizabeth, Gloria and Muriel;
Ida, Lizzie, and Ella; and Elizabeth Ashton

Quotes & Excerpts

"A nation is not conquered..."
    –Traditional Cheyenne

"It's time for the women to pick up their medicine..."
    –Art Solomon, from a speech at the Native Canadian Centre of
    Toronto, fall 1989.

"I am not your princess..."
    –Chrystos, from *Not Vanishing*, Press Gang, 1988.

"...the concept of betraying one's race through sex and sexual
politics..."
    –Cherríe Moraga, from *Loving in the War Years*, South End Press,
    1983.

"What I want is the freedom to carve and chisel my own face..."
    –Gloria Anzaldúa, from *Borderlands/La Frontera*, Spinsters/Aunt
    Lute Book Company, 1987.

"...we embrace and rub the wounds together..."
"This ain't no stoic look..."
    –Diane Burns, from *Riding the One–Eyed Ford*, Contact II
    Publications, 1981.

"The Word Warriors"
    –Paula Gunn Allen, from *The Sacred Hoop*, Beacon Press, 1986.

"...I am here to speak for my brother and my brother-in-law..."
    –Kayapo woman, from transcription of *The Nature of Things* with
    David Suzuki, Show #19, "Amazonia–The Road to the End of the
    Forest," CBC, 1989–1990.

Excerpt from *Star Boy* by Robert Priest and Bongo Herbert, G'tel
Records and Tapes, 1984.

Excerpt from *You light Up My Life* by Joe Brooks, Big Hill Music Corp.,
1976, 1977.

Production Notes

PRINCESS POCAHONTAS AND THE BLUE SPOTS was developed through grants from the Canada Council, the Ontario Arts Council and the Toronto Arts Council. It was originally workshopped by Monique Mojica and Alejandra Nuñez with direction and dramaturgy by Djanet Sears beginning in the spring of 1988. It was subsequently workshopped by Nightwood Theatre in a co-production with Native Earth Performing Arts in May 1989, directed by Muriel Miguel with dramaturgy by Djanet Sears and Kate Lushington, and was read at the Weesageechak Festival of New Work by Native Playwrights in the Backspace of Theatre Passe Muraille in June 1989. It was presented as a work in progress at the Groundswell Festival of New Work by Women produced by Nightwood Theatre in November 1989, directed by Djanet Sears, and was fully produced at the Theatre Passe Muraille Backspace in co-production with Nightwood Theatre from February 9 to March 4, 1990.

Credits

Performers:	Monique Mojica
	Alejandra Nuñez
Director:	Muriel Miguel
Original Music and Lyrics:	Alejandra Nuñez
Lyrics:	*"The Ballad of Princess Pocahontas"*
	"En Tulum Canta La Luna" and
	"Captain Whiteman" by Monique Mojica
Set and Lighting Design:	Stephan Droege
Props and Costume Design:	Pat Mohan
Stage Manager:	Sandra McEwing
Dramaturge:	Djanet Sears
Producers:	Nightwood Theatre and
	Theatre Passe Muraille

Character Descriptions

Played by Monique Mojica:

Princess Buttered-on-Both-Sides

One of the many faces of the Trickster, Coyote. She is a contestant in the Miss North American Indian Beauty Pageant and she is stuck in the talent segment.

Contemporary Woman #1

A modern, Native woman on a journey to recover the history of her grandmothers as a tool towards her own healing.

Malinche

A Nahuatl woman who was the interpreter and strategist for the Spanish conquistador, Hernán Cortez. She was also his mistress and bore him one son. Throughout Mexico and much of Latin America, she is referred to as "La Chingada" - the fucked one, and her name is synomynous with traitor. In some legends, Malinche turns into a volcano when Cortez leaves Mexico.

Storybook Pocahontas

The little Indian Princess from the picture books, friend of the settlers, in love with the Captain, comes complete with her savage-Indian-Chief father.

Pocahontas/Lady Rebecca/Matoaka

The three names of Pocahontas, a Powhatan woman whose father was the chief of the Powhatan Confederacy at the time of the Jamestown Colony in Virginia. She is best known for saving the life of Captain John Smith when she was eleven years old, and for saving the colonists from starvation. The legendary Pocahontas of the ballads and romantic poetry has become the archetype of the "good Indian:" one who aids and abets white men. Lady Rebecca was what she was named when she was Christianized and married John Rolfe. Matoaka was her name as a child.

Deity/Woman of the Puna/Virgin

Written for the female deities who have been usurped by the Catholic church and turned into virgins. Deity's name could be Nusta Huillac, Tonatzin, Coyolahuaxqui or many others. Woman of the Puna was a Quechua woman who along with others, refused to become Christianized, left the Spanish court of colonial Peru and fled to the high tablelands of the Andes called the *puna* where they lived without men. This area is still considered woman's territory. In this tradition there were also virgin priestesses who were married to the sun. La Virgen del Carmen (La Tirana), and La Virgen de Guadelupe are only two of the Catholic virgins to whom devotion was built upon already existing reverence to female deities and leaders.

Marie/Margaret/Madelaine
Three faces out of the hordes of Cree and Métis women who portaged across Canada with white men on their backs and were then systemically discarded.

Cigar Store Squaw
Princess Buttered on Both Sides embodies another well-known and accepted icon of Native Women.

Spirit Animal
The one who travels with you; she guides, guards and protects.

Played by Alejandra Nuñez:

Host
The beauty pageant M.C., a cross between Bert Parks and a sleazy Latin band leader.

The Blue Spots
The "doo-wop" girls who back up Princess Pocahontas and her band.

Contemporary Woman#2
A modern Chilean-born woman who carries her history of resistance from the survival of the Andean women, to the "Amanda" guerrilleras to her own story as a refugee. As a woman of the Americas, she accompanies Contemporary Woman#1 on her journey.

Troubador
The entertainer in the Elizabethan court upon Pocahontas' arrival in England.

Ceremony
The personification of the puberty ritual. She is the instructions of the grandmothers, she is the fast, she is the songs, she is the

> dance, she is the paint, she is the sacred blood, she is the initiation.

The Man

> The husband, the lover, the friend, the "brother" in the struggle whose oppression is fully understood but whom the women end up carrying anyway.

Spirit-Sister

> A helper, a guide, an equal on the other side.

Musician

> Plays sampoñas, guitar, tiple, drums, pennywhistle, ocarinas, and birimbao as well as a variety of small percussion instruments and vocals.

Note on structure, transformations and transfigurations:

There are 13 transformations, one for each moon in the lunar year. These transformations can sometimes be very sudden or they can linger and evolve gradually.

There are 4 sections where there is a transfiguration of three women or entities who are one.

This is the inherent structure of the play, it is not a structure that was imposed on the story, but rather, a structure that was informed by the characters. This means that I didn't realize that I had a "structure" until I went through the process of preparing the manuscript for publication. I learned a lot about trusting my own way of working.

13 moons, 4 directions; it is not a linear structure but it is the form and the basis from which these stories must be told.

Set Description

The theme of the set, costumes and props is also transformation; objects and set pieces appear to be one thing but become something else; they can be turned inside-out to reveal another reality. The pile of cloth becomes a garment, a canal, a volcano; the gilded portrait frame is pulled away from the wall where it has been camouflaged in the foliage of the tree and the rainforest; the pyramid becomes the staircase of a Vegas-style show; and the limbs of the tree of life can be a playground or a place from which to hang oneself.

The tree stands upstage right and is draped in layers of fabric in luxurious textures, there is a platform at the crotch of the tree and it is hollow. At the foot of the tree are placed an enamel basin, cup and pitcher of water, a small pot of red paint, a bucket of sand, and a bag of popcorn. There is a pyramid upstage left with stairs facing both downstage and stage right. A pole downstage left is pegged for climbing and decorated with the faces and clothing of the Métis women. At the base of the pole is an enamel basin of water. At the beginning of the show the stage is bare except for these things and the volcano/cloth placed downstage left and draped along the circle which is centrestage and painted to look like a copper disk. At the end of the show the stage is littered with debris from the stories that are told.

Transformation 1
500 years of the Miss North American Indian Beauty Pageant

The stage is empty. As the lights go to black, CONTEMPORARY
WOMAN #2 *jumps into spotlight as beauty pageant* HOST.

HOST: Good evening ladies and gentlemen, and children of all
ages and welcome to the 498th annual – count them – that's
nearly 500 years of the **Miss North American Indian
Beauty Pageant!** This is George Pepe Flaco Columbus
Cartier da Gama Smith, but you can call me Bob, coming to
you live from the Indian Princess Hall of Fame.

Crosses centre.

Our first contestant in the Miss North American Indian
Beauty pageant, from her home in the deep green forest on
the other side of the mountain, by the shores of the silver
sea – Princess Buttered-on-Both-Sides!!

HOST *begins to "oooo" the first line from the 'Indian Love Call'
which is echoed by* PRINCESS BUTTERED-ON-BOTH-SIDES *as she
enters dressed in a white "buckskin" dress and carrying an over-
sized ear of corn. As she weaves through audience, she offers them
handfuls of cornnuts from the plastic bag she bought them in.*

PRINCESS BUTTERED-ON-BOTH-SIDES:
Corn... Corn... Corn... Corn...

*The music is a mixture of Hollywood 'tom-toms', the 'Indian
Love Call', 'The Good, the Bad and the Ugly' and the "Mazola'
commercial.*

PRINCESS BUTTERED-ON-BOTH-SIDES:
(to audience) Excuse me, which way is east? *(after a member
of the audience answers)* Many, many thanks.

PRINCESS BUTTERED-ON-BOTH-SIDES *tosses cornnuts to the four
directions and places her ear to the earth, she rises, arms and face
lifted to the heavens in a classic "spiritual" Hollywood Indian pose.*

PRINCESS BUTTERED-ON-BOTH-SIDES:

> *(pointing to the ear of corn)* Corn.
>
> *(pointing to herself)* Maiden.
>
> For the talent segment of the Miss North American Indian Beauty Pageant, I shall dance for you, in savage splendour, the "Dance of the Sacrificial Corn Maiden", and proceed to hurl myself over the precipice, all for the loss of my one true love, CAPTAIN JOHN WHITEMAN. *(swoons)*
>
> *Music starts up. The production number is from the movie "Rosemarie" – corn celebration – played on pan pipes with vocalized cartoon sound effects. Princess Buttered-on-Both-Sides performs a Hollywood 'Injun dance'.*

PRINCESS BUTTERED-ON-BOTH-SIDES:

> *(teetering on the edge of the 'precipice' or stage)* OH, that's Niagara Falls down there, but I just can't live without him!
>
> *Teeters but is saved by the music beginning again.* PRINCESS BUTTERED-ON-BOTH-SIDES *dances again, removes the buckskin dress and runs to the edge of the precipice once more. She jumps.*

> **GERONIMOOOOOOOOO!!!!!**

Transformation 2
On the Precipice

Scuttling around circle, on hands and knees, searching.

CONTEMPORARY WOMAN #1:

> No map, no trail, no footprint, no way home
> > only darkness, a cold wind whistling by my ears.
>
> The only light comes from the stars.
> > Nowhere to set my feet.
> > > no place to stand. *(rising)*
>
> No map, no trail, no footprint , no way home.
>
> *Sees basin of water; brings it to center.*

He said, "It's time for the women to pick up their medicine in order for the people to continue." *(washes hands, arms)*

She asked him, " What is the women's medicine?" The only answer he found was, "The women are the medicine, so we must heal the women.

Washes from basin head, arms, legs, feet. Tiple theme begins.

Squatting over basin in a birthing position, she lifts a newborn from between her legs, holding baby in front of her, she rises.

When I was born, the umbilical cord was wrapped
    around my neck and my face was blue.
When I was born, my mother turned me over to
    check for the blue spot at the base of the spine –
    the sign of Indian blood.
When my child was born, after counting the fingers
    and the toes, I turned it over to check for the blue
    spot at the base of the spine.
Even among the half-breeds, it's one of the last
    things to go.

CONTEMPORARY WOMAN #2:
    Princess, Princess!

CONTEMPORARY WOMAN #1:
    Princess, Princess!

CONTEMPORARY WOMAN #2:

Princess, Princess Amazon Queen.
Show me your royal blood,
Is it blue? Is it green?
Dried and brown five centuries old,
singed and baked and
covered with mold?

CONTEMPORARY WOMAN #1:
(on 'singed')
Le le le le le le le le le
    le le le le le
one little, two little,
    three little...
no sound no flutter
    no movement.

CONTEMPORARY WOMAN #2:

>Princess, priestess Caribe Queen,
>What are you selling today,
>Is it corn, tobacco, beans?
>Snake oil or a beaver hat.
>Horse liniment,
>you can't beat that!

CONTEMPORARY WOMAN #1:
(on 'liniment', singing)
ee ge bee ba ne bo e
   bo e bua
ta le ma la ye
"I am a Starboy
I shoot through the night
In a rocket of silver
That sails on light."

CONTEMPORARY WOMAN #2:

>Princess, Princess, calendar girl,
>Redskin temptress, Indian pearl.
>Waiting by the water
>for a white man to save.
>She's a savage now remember –
>Can't behave!

CONTEMPORARY WOMAN #1:
(on 'she's a savage')
"I am not your Princess ...
I am only willing to tell you
how to make fry bread."

>*(singing)*

My black jack daisy
win na ya hey yo
She got mad at me
because I said hello.

>*(speaking)*

"...the concept of
betraying one's race
through sex and
   sexual politics
is as common as corn."

CONTEMPORARY WOMAN #2:

>Princess, Princess

CONTEMPORARY WOMAN #1:

>Princess, Princess

BOTH: Are you a real Indian Princess?

>CONTEMPORARY WOMAN #1 *and* #2 *stand together downstage centre, extend their hands, arms feeling the shift in air. They breathe energy downstage, upstage, stageleft and stageright until the breath becomes sound and they separate into spirals in opposite directions.* CONTEMPORARY WOMAN #2 *exits.*

Transformation 3

Invocation

As each woman, group of women or spirit is named, she is placed at each of the four directions in the following order: (counter-clockwise). East, North, West, South. MALINCHE *also arrives from the South and overtakes* CONTEMPORARY WOMAN #1. *The name becomes* MALINCHE'S *wail as she is cursed.*

CONTEMPORARY WOMAN #1:
Pocahontas.
The women who birthed the Métis.
(surprise) Coyote?
The women of the Puna.

Ocarina music, on tape.

Malinche ... Malinche? **MALINCHE!!**

CONTEMPORARY WOMAN #2:
Puta! Chingada! Cabrona! India de mierda!
Hija de tu mala madre! Maldita Malinche!

She curses and spits at MALINCHE, *exits to instruments.*

CONTEMPORARY WOMAN #1 *receives each curse as a wound, she furiously hurls herself onto the heap of cloth downstage left and speaks as* MALINCHE.

MALINCHE: They say it was me betrayed my people. It was they betrayed me!

MUSICIAN: *(singing with tape)*
Santa Maria, Santa Maria, Santa Malinche.

MALINCHE *crawls backwards on her stomach; picks up cloth/volcano and rises to her knees.*

MALINCHE: You spit my name. My name is Malinali. Not Doña Marina, not Malinche, La Chingada! The fucked one! *(rises with cloth/volcano as a skirt)* What is my curse? *(runs stageright)* My blood cursed you with your broad face? *(whips cloth causing it to billow; volcano now is at waist height)* Eyes set wide apart? Black hair? Your wide square feet? Or the blue spot you wear on your butt when you're born? *(backs up, stamping feet rhythmically)* You are the child planted in me by Hernán Cortez who begins the bastard race, born from La Chingada! You deny me? *(whips volcano, throws it over her head, emerges from under it, downstage right)* I wear the face of Malinali Tenepat. I see this face reflected in the mirror. Mirror my eyes reflecting back at me. Reflecting words. It is my words he wants you see... I am the only one can speak to the Maya, to the Mexica. It is my words that are of value. *(moves downstage right, crosses herself, kneeling with head bowed)* I am christened Doña Marina. They call me "Princess". I am a gift, claimed as value by this man in metal. I can change the words. I have power. Now I ride at the side of Cortez, the lady of the conquistador. Smart woman. I am a strategist. Dangerous woman. *(walking backwards, swirling volcano/cloth with feet, sits upstage left)*

MUSICIAN: *(singing)*
Santa Maria,
Santa Marina,
Santa Malinche.
Hija de puta, traidora.

MALINCHE: *(on 'Marina', gathering edges of volcano/cloth)*
On this shell I sit,
holding the net,
keeping the balance,
watching,
hearing everything –

MUSICIAN: *(shouts)* Traitor! Whore!

MALINCHE: – and they hardly see me (Oh) look at them. The Spaniards all wear armour and clothing that's heavy and dark and they sweat in their heavy clothes and their hairy bodies.

Rises, picks up volcano/cloth, holds it like a dress against her body.

This morning I told those girls who help me dress to braid my hair tightly, and coil it around my head like two snakes. I didn't want any pieces falling in my face, nothing to distract me. I knew I'd have to listen very hard.

Picks up volcano/cloth, holding it by the hoop at chest level, she walks up ramp to pyramid upstage left.

MUSICIAN: *(singing, dissonant)* Santa Maria, Santa Marina, Santa Malinche...

MALINCHE: *Retreats backwards up ramp upstage left, then whips cloth/volcano, so it writhes.*

What is that they say about me?

That I opened my legs to the whole conquering Spanish army? They were already here. I was a gift. Passed on. Handed on. Like so many pounds of gold bullion, dragged out of the earth, dragged out of the treasure rooms of Moctezuma. Stolen! Bound! Caught! Trapped!

Hands volcano to MUSICIAN *who secures it to the side of the set so that it cascades down onto the stage.* MALINCHE *scrambles up pyramid, crawls haltingly down other side.*

The night called La Noche Triste. We have to leave Tenochtitlan. Moctezuma and his children are dead. Whose sad night is it? The bridge has to be carried. Forty men. And the noise... They've found us out, that we are leaving. *(running behind tree and down the stageright ramp)* Cortez and I go over first and then the rest of them.*(rolling underneath the volcano/cloth, punching and flailing)* And the screaming and the horses falling in the canals and we have to run. *(emerging through slit in volcano/cloth to standing)* I look back, I see the canals piled high with bodies – bodies piled so high. *(arching spine and rolling onto cloth on floor, folling sinking gold)* They are crossed by climbing over the bodies, as the gold sinks to the bottom of the canals. *(as if wiping blood from her hands)* It didn't matter how brave the warriors nor how strong the weapons.

You say it was me betrayed my people, but it was they betrayed me!

MUSICIAN: *Singing, as* MALINCHE *climbs the pyramid nearly to the top and takes volcano.*

Puta, chingada, cabrona, India de mierda, hija de tu mala madre, maldita Malinche.

MALINCHE: *Sits at top of pyramid, whipping volcano into raging flows of lava*

I spit, burn and char the earth. A net of veins binding me to you as I am bound to this piece of earth. So bound.

A volcano, this woman. *(stands, volcano/cloth at shoulder level)*
I turn to tree whose branches drip bleeding flowers. Bleed
into this piece of earth where I grow, mix with volcanic ash
and produce fertile soil. Born from the earth, fed with my
blood, anything alive here is alive because I stayed alive!

I turn to wind. You hear my Llorona's wail screaming
across the desert.

Lost in the rain forest, you remember –

Malinche!!—

She wails, raising the volcano/cloth up over her head.

Transformation 4

Live from Tee Pee Town

From underneath volcano/cloth MUSICIAN *joins* PRINCESS
BUTTERED-ON-BOTH-SIDES *as the* SACRIFICIAL VIRGIN, *hooking
her arms through* VIRGIN'S *from behind. All hand movements are*
MUSICIAN'S. *As they rise from within the volcano, only* VIRGIN'S
face is seen lip-synching as MUSICIAN'S *voice transforms the
'wail' into Ima Sumac's, "Las Virgenes del Sol," sung in
operatic style. Then becomes the voice of live, bubbling lava deep
within the volcano.*

MUSICIAN: Um woka, woka, woka... Um woka, woka, woka...

VIRGIN: Oh - oh...

MUSICIAN: Um woka, woka... Um woka, woka... JUMP!

VIRGIN: NO!

MUSICIAN: Um woka, woka... Um woka, woka... *(mimes diving motion)*

VIRGIN: Have you got the wrong virgin!

MUSICIAN: Um woka, woka... JUMP NOW!

VIRGIN: I think I left something on the stove. *Exits with volcano leaving* MUSICIAN *crouched and exposed.*

MUSICIAN: Um woka, woka, woka... *(realizing she is exposed, begins her 50's style 'doo wops')*

Boom ba boom ba - ba boom... ba boom ba - ba boom... *Flourishing to an entrance cue for* PRINCESS-BUTTERED-ON-BOTH-SIDES; *who does not enter.*

PRINCESS BUTTERED-ON-BOTH-SIDES:
(loud stage whisper; offstage) NOT YET!

MUSICIAN: *Nervously repeats 'doo wops' with entrance cue; no entrance.*

PRINCESS BUTTERED-ON-BOTH-SIDES:
(loud stage whisper; offstage) It's the velcro!

MUSICIAN: *Repeats doo wop intro, confidently now, with entrance cue.*

PRINCESS BUTTERED-ON-BOTH-SIDES:
(show-biz entrance with hand-held mike) Live from Tee Pee Town...it's Princess Pocahontas and the Blue Spots!

BLUE SPOTS: Shoo bee, doo bee, wa!

PRINCESS BUTTERED-ON-BOTH-SIDES:
(a la Marilyn Monroe) Way ya hiya!

Descends pyramid and they sing with a drawling country and western feel, the BLUE SPOTS *do-wopping for all they are worth.*

Captain Whiteman, I would pledge my life to you
Captain Whiteman, I would defy my father too.
I pledge to aid and to save,
I'll protect you to my grave.
Oh Captain Whiteman, you're the cheese in my fondue.

Captain Whiteman for you, I will convert,
Captain Whiteman, all my pagan gods are dirt.
If I'm savage don't despise me,
'cause I'll let you civilize me.
Oh Captain Whiteman, I'm your buckskin clad dessert.

Although you may be hairy,
I love you so-oo,
You're the cutestest guy I'll ever see.
You smell a little funny,
But don't you worry, honey,

come live with me in my tee pee.

Captain Whiteman, I'm a little Indian maid,
Captain Whiteman, with a long ebony braid.
Please don't let my dark complexion
Inhibit your affection.
Be my muffin, I'll be your marmalade.
Be my muffin, I'll be your marmalade.
Be my muffin, I'll be your marmalade.
Way ya hey yo.

During muffin refrain, the **Blue Spots** *run up centre aisle,*
screaming

BLUE SPOTS: ¡Capitan! ¡Capitan! ¡No te vayas, Capitan! Don't leave me!

PRINCESS BUTTERED-ON-BOTH-SIDES:

May you always walk in beauty, my dear sister.

Now, was that not spiritual? Many, many thanks, you have
made my heart soar like the noble rabbit. My heart, your
heart, bunny heart, one heart. Um hmm.

I would like us to be friends, real good friends, you know
what I mean? I mean like blood brothers, and blood sisters.
Um hm.

I have many names. My first name was Matoaka. Some
people call me Lady Rebecca, but everyone knows the little
Indian Princess Pocahontas, who saved the life of Captain
John Smith.

Transformation 5

Storybook Pocahontas

Four gestures, once through no words, once with sounds, once
with text.

STORYBOOK POCAHONTAS:

1) NO! *(hands overhead, on knees)* He's so brave his eyes are
so blue, his hair is so blond and I like the way he walks.

2) DON'T! *(arms cradling Captain's head)* Mash his brain out!
I don't want to see his brains all running down the side of
this stone.

3) STOP! *(in the name of love)* I think I love him.

4) Oooh *(swooning, hands at cheeks)* He's so cute.

Removes Princess dress, stands downstage right.

CONTEMPORARY WOMAN #1:
> *(to audience)* Where was her mother?

ambivilance

Transformation 6
Pocahontas/Lady Rebecca/Matoaka Transfiguration

TROUBADOUR:
> *(complete with Robin Hood hat, singing:)*
> In 1607 the English came sailing
>   across the ocean –
> In the name of their virgin queen,
>   they called this land Virginia-O.
>
> (STORYBOOK POCAHONTAS *joins)*
>
> In the gloom and silence of the dark
>   and impenetrable forest-
> They might all have died if it had not been
>   for the Indian Princess Pocahontas-O.
>
> Her father was a stern, old chief,
>   Powhatan was his name-O
> Sweet and pretty was Pocahontas
>   As he was ugly and cruel-O.
>
> Then into her village strode a man
>   with steps so brave and sure-
> Said he in a deep voice like a God's
>   "My name is Captain John Smith-O

> *chorus*
> Heigh-ho wiggle-waggle
>   wigwam wampum,
>   roly-poly papoose tom-tom,
>   tomahawk squaw.

LADY REBECCA:
> How camst I here? I know how to walk, I know how to
> stand, I know how to incline my head, how to bow.
> *(grand curtsey)* My heart is on the ground!

STORYBOOK POCAHONTAS & TROUBADOUR:
> The fiendish red men they did deem
>   that John Smith he must die-O
> They placed his head upon a stone,
>   and raised their tomahawks high-O.
>
> Then from the crowd there rushed a girl,
>   the maiden Pocahontas
> Shielding his head with her own ,
>   crying save him save the Paleface-O.
>
> *chorus*
> Heigh-ho wiggle-waggle
>   wigwam wampum,
>   roly-poly papoose tom-tom,
>   tomahawk squaw.

LADY REBECCA:
> *Crosses to wall stage right, swings out larger-than-life gilded
> portrait frame which contains* LADY REBECCA'S *lace ruff, cuffs
> and velvet hat with an ostrich plume.*
>
> How camst I to be caught, stuck, girdled? I'll tell you
> Captain,
>
> John Smith: "You did promise Powhatan that what was
> yours should be his, and he the like to you; you called him
> father. And fear you here I should call you father? I tell you
> then, I will, and you shall call me child, and so I will be
> forever and ever your countryman. They did tell us always
> (that) you were dead, and I knew no other until I came to
> Plymouth. Yet Powhatan did seek to know the truth,
> because your countrymen will lie much."

TROUBADOUR: *(singing)*
>When Pocahontas went to see her friend
>John Smith in Jamestown-
>She'd run and cartwheel with the boys,
>though she be naked underneath it-O.
>
>John Smith said of the Indian girls
>"I could have done what I listed"-O
>"All these nymphs more tormented me,
>crying 'Love you not me? Love you not me?'"

During these verses LADY REBECCA *caresses clothing in frame.*

LADY REBECCA:
>Now see you here, I wear the clothes of an Englishwoman
>and will disturb you less when I walk. Here, I am Princess
>and Non Pareil of Virigina. I am Lady Rebecca. For me the
>Queen holds audience. Treachery, Captain, I was kidnapped!

TROUBADOUR: *(singing)*
>There chanc'd to be in Jamestown
>   a planter named John Rolfe-O
>His heart was touched by Pocahontas
>   he claimed her for his bride-y-O.

LADY REBECCA:
>John, my husband, is a businessman, a merchant and a
>tobacco planter. I know how to grow tobacco, it is our
>sacred tobacco plant.

TROUBADOUR: *(singing and marching with drum; a funeral dirge)*
>Yo sangro por ti... yo sangro por ti...
>sangro... sangro... sangro...

Continues under Apostle's Creed: live voice and drum layered over taped voices.

LADY REBECCA:
>*Fitting neck and wrists into collar and cuffs with much
>resistance as if being put into stocks and pillory; fanning herself
>with ostrich plume fan.*
>
>I believe in God the Father Almighty, maker of Heaven and
>Earth, and in Jesus Christ his only son our Lord, who was
>conceived of the Holy Ghost, born of the Virgin Mary,

suffered under Pontius Pilate, was crucified, dead and buried. He descended into hell. I believe in the Holy Ghost, the holy Catholic Church, the communion of saints, the forgiveness of sins, the resurrection of the body and the life everlasting. Amen. *(music out)*

I provided John Rolfe with the seeds to create his hybrid tobacco plants and I provided him with a son, and created a hybrid people. I have such a nice fan to hide my face and fan myself in these hot, heavy clothes.

What owe I to my father? Waited I not one year in Jamestown, a prisoner? One year before sent he my brothers to seek me. "If my father had loved me, he would not value me less than old swords, guns or axes: therefore I shall still dwell with the Englishmen who love me."

Can I still remember how to plant corn? I'll stay. Never, never go back where anyone might know Matoaka. My name is Lady Rebecca forever and always. I am a Christian Englishwoman!

TROUBADOUR: *(singing)*
> Alas for our dear lady,
>> English climate did not suit her–
> She never saw Virginia again,
>> she met her end at Gravesend.

LADY REBECCA:
> Says John, my husband:

> For the good of God, for the good of the country, for the good of the plantation. It is righteous and it is good.

> No mark, no trail, no footprint, no way home. *(reaching through frame, throwing a lifeline across the generations)*

> It is enough that the child liveth!

TROUBADOUR: *(singing, joined by* STORYBOOK POCAHONTAS*)*
> And so here ends the legend
>> of the Princess Pocahontas–
> Fa la la la lay, fa la la la la LELF–
>> if you want any more, make it up yourself.
>>> *chorus*

> Heigh-ho wiggle-waggle
>   wigwam wampum,
>   roly-poly papoose tom-tom
>   tomahawk squaw.

MATOAKA runs to the tree upstage right, climbs half-way up, peeks around tree trunk.

MATOAKA: I belong to the deer clan – *(climbing onto platform in tree)*

That's my family. We're the only ones can wear deer antlers when we dance our deer clan dance. We have to dance running as fast as the deer, kick up our feet, sniff the air.

I belong to the deer clan.

This is the first year I'll dance with the other girls. My first deer dance. My mother says, I have to have my own paint that's only mine. *(climbing down tree)* So I have to find my own colours and mix my own paint. My mother says I have to wait until I know and I'm really sure that that's how I want my face to be. Because that will be my paint and my face forever. It's very important. *(sits, upstage centre)*

Enter CEREMONY downstage left with birimbao; she plays birimbao and keeps rhythm with her feet, dancing throughout 'Nubile Child' whose cadence is chanted to the rhythm of the birimbao.

MATOAKA: Nubile child. Nubile child thigh strong muscle in the sun
back to the sun woman/child –
Nubile child work in the corn
basket on her back in the sun. Basket on her back.
Nubile child strong rain woman/child fix the roof
woman/child.
Nubile child water from the river sun on the water
open up look up!
See your face in the water, hand in your hair
woman/child – laugh
Wet your auntie's basket!
Nubile child swimming, not working, nubile child.
Strong, fast, free *(jumps up, runs downstage right)*
woman/child-digging –

Backing up into circle, back to back with CEREMONY.

digging with a stick, find the right roots,
Put them in your basket woman/child.
Name of the flower, name of the leaf, which one for
headaches,
which one for broken bones, which one to pray, which ones
never to touch... (never to touch never to touch never to
touch).

(to CEREMONY *who doesn't look at her)*

And I'm the first one of my sisters to be old enough to
dance with the others.

My brothers are teasing me. That's because they know it's
important. And you can't laugh. *(laughing, runs up tree,
climbs around back of tree while speaking)*

It means I'll be a woman now. It means I'll have different
work.

It means there are some things I won't be able to do like the
little girls. It means that soon I'll be ready to be a wife.

*Slides down ramp, upstage right; bounces on knees to rhythm
then rises to centrestage.*

Becoming woman/child – open up/Look!
All around your world,everything's alive!
Everything is growing, *(embraces tree)* everything has spirit,
everything is breathing, *(kneels, washes hands in basin at tree)*
everything needs water, everything needs sunlight,
everything needs rest.

*Reaches for pot of red paint from base of tree; in four gestures,
paints outer arms, and the tops of both feet with red paint,
prepared for initiation, she stands and dances toward* CEREMONY
upstage centre.

MATOAKA: Nubile child,

CEREMONY: *(echoes)* Nubile child,

MATOAKA: strong, fast, free woman/child
strong legs, brown skin, woman/child
Look all the way around you. *(dances downstage centre)*
Look around your world woman/child

(stops dancing; very still)

Dark skies, the moon is mine
stars travel
woman's time.

Transformation 7
Deity/Woman of the Puna/Virgin Transfiguration

> CONTEMPORARY WOMAN #1 *carries basin downstage centre onto ramp. Sits; offers water with her hand; washes feet stands and starts up ramp with basin, noticing that she is leaving footprints behind her, she stops, and follows them with her eyes.*

DEITY: Let me tell you how I became a virgin:
I was the warrior woman
rebel woman
creator/destroyer
womb of the earth
mother of all
– married to none
but the sun himself
or maybe the Lord of the underworld.
My butterfly wings transform
are reborn into flight as
Grandmother Spiderwoman
spins the threads of stories
as I tell them to you.

MUSICIAN: *(singing with guitar)*
Quisiera...
Because... every step you took was to
destroy my world, and as long as I breathe;
you'll never find your way through jungles
of thoughts,to see my eyes again...
to see my eyes again...
Quisiera...

DEITY: I wore a serpent skirt
between my breasts skulls dangle
ornamenting   my power   and
whetting   your fear.
Of my membranes muscle blood and bone I
birthed a continent
– because I thought –
and creation came to be.

Walks up ramp to downstage right.

I was the leader with the iron fist
the renegade.
You never knew if I was abducted or
ran of my own
free will
to the
Spanish miner/Portugese sailor-man
(or maybe it was the
other way around)?

WOMAN OF THE PUNA:

Turns upstage, offering basin to tree.

Defiant, I refused to turn my back on
the mother ways.
Betrayed by our own fathers brothers uncles
husbands... *(places basin at tree)*
We run to the puna – *(runs up into tree)*

(from platform)

In the high tablelands
my sisters and I
refuse to weep, *(stands with rope noose in hands)*
our eyes, instead, spit fire. *(drum begins; tape)*
We, in secret, herd together, *(sampoñas; live, inside tree)*
honor the mother,
live without men,
demand our purity be
reclaimed.
We hung ourselves, slit our throats,
cut the breath of
our male children.

VIRGIN: Let me tell you then, how I became a virgin.
          Separated from myself my balance destroyed,
          scrubbed clean
          made lighter, non threatening
          chaste   barren.
          No longer allied with the darkness
          of moon tides
          but twisted and misaligned
          with the darkness of evil
          the invaders sinful apple
          in my hand!
          Nusta Huillac! La Tirana! La Virgen del Carmen...
          Tonantzin! Coyolahuaxquil The Dark Virgin of
          Guadalupe...
          Draped in ribbons, lace and flowers
          we are carried through the streets
          Stripped – of our names
          and our light
          Let me tell you how I became a virgin,

          Slowly lowering noose; resisting it.

          Sexless, without fire
          without pleasure
          without power
          Encased in plaster
          painted white.
          But oh, if there is one child
          who sees my nostrils flare
          my eyes spark and
          recognizes the heartbeat
          from the stomping of my feet
          in the rattle of the snare drum.

          Sampoñas fade; snare drum continues under CONTEMPORARY
          WOMAN #2.

CONTEMPORARY WOMAN #2:
          (upstage centre; standing)
          And when Amanda would go to visit her man, her
          compañero, in jail, she would be strip-searched. In order to
          smuggle liquor or alcohol for their wounds, anything that

would bring some comfort into the prison, she would fill little bottles, and hide them in her vagina –
– the perfect hiding place.

Resumes playing sampoñas.

Transformation 8

Grandfathers/Stand Up

CONTEMPORARY WOMAN #1 *crosses to ramp stage left wrapping herself luxuriously in volcano/cloth, sampoñas continue under.*

CONTEMPORARY WOMAN #1:

Sometimes, when you are not with me, I pull long, long strands of black hair, that doesn't belong to me, from between my sheets, from between the pages of my notebooks.

CONTEMPORARY WOMAN #2:

From between my sheets... the pages of my notebooks...

CONTEMPORARY WOMAN #1:

Your profile a silhouette against the mid-day sun,
I watch you pluck whiskers with a tweezers.
I remember my grandfather sitting in the
sun of a soot-streaked city window, plucking whiskers,
grazing his face with a scissors, smiling at me from the side
of his mouth.
You smile a crooked smile, embarrassed that I see them in
you – all my grandfathers; those short, dark men with
broad shoulders and heavy muscled calves, with hard
working feet that were made for climbing coconut trees
and walking in the sand; their pigeon-toed gait out of time
on the sidewalks of the city.

As sampoñas resume, CONTEMPORARY WOMAN #1 *runs stage right, searching for the sound.*

I followed the sound of the drum until I found where it was coming from. What was the sound of pipes doing in this northern market? *(centrestage)* You didn't know who I was, and it was months before I could explain to you that this woman, so exhilarated by the sound of the sikus, the pipes, the camu, was feeling the sound running through her veins!

(downstage centre) I remember my grandfathers sitting in my grandmother's front parlour, Sunday afternoons, playing the camu – blowing across the bamboo pipes. Iieeeeee! Iieeeeee!

One of them would start to cry — a high-pitched wail. The others would tease and laugh, but one by one they'd join his cry: a brotherhood of old, brown men mourning their lost home; a sorrowful sound whose bass note is a conch shell blown far out over the water.

You tilt your face to the sky, arch your back, bring the shell to your lips and blow. From the rumble at the soles of my feet to the insistent vibration at the top of my head,

I recognize the sound. *(sampuñus stop)*

Moves to pot of paint upstage right and in one deliberate gesture, paints the centre part in her hair; returns downstage centre.

I recognize my lifeline in your face when you bow your head in respect to hold a single kernel of corn in your hand; and Grandpa planted corn in the backyard. *(sinks to knees)*

THE MAN: *(crosses downstage centre to* CONTEMPORARY WOMAN #1; *touches shoulder)*
Parase Negrita, vamos. Mira toda la gente que vino

CONTEMPORARY WOMAN #1 *stands; looks at* THE MAN, *both look at audience, smile.* THE MAN *buckles and falls to his knees.*

CONTEMPORARY WOMAN #1:
Stand up! Look, you are my man, I am your woman. Stand up.

THE MAN: Right on.

CONTEMPORARY WOMAN #1:
We, native women, are the centre of the hoop of the nation.

THE MAN: *Falls.*

CONTEMPORARY WOMAN #1:
>Stand up! *(helping him to stand)* Stand up on your own two feet. You have two feet *(points)* one, two. Stand up.

THE MAN: *Nods, in agreement.*

CONTEMPORARY WOMAN #1:
>We are like the earth, we are the backbone...

THE MAN: *Falls sideways, climbs onto* CONTEMPORARY WOMAN #1's *back.*

CONTEMPORARY WOMAN #1:
>... and when our warriors go out to fight, we quietly support them. *(to* THE MAN*)* Not on my back! the baby's up there!
>Stand up and walk next to me!

THE MAN: *Nods, affirmative.*

CONTEMPORARY WOMAN #1:
>Now, there is a war being waged on the cement prairie and...

THE MAN: *Crossing downstage of* CONTEMPORARY WOMAN #1, *following someone hungrily with eyes.*

CONTEMPORARY WOMAN #1:
>Hey, where're you... ? Not with that white woman over there! *(grabs* THE MAN *by both arms and shakes him)* We're supposed to be re-building the nations, **RIGHT**??

THE MAN: *Falls.*

CONTEMPORARY WOMAN #1:
>*(helping him to stand)* Stand up. Please stand up. Pleeaase stand up?

THE MAN: *Standing tall.*

CONTEMPORARY WOMAN #1:
>There!

THE MAN: *Now that he is standing tall, he exits upstage left.*

CONTEMPORARY WOMAN #1:
>Hey! Hey where are you going? I don't want to do this without you! Hey! Hey!

Transformation 9
Marie/Margaret/Madelaine – Métis women Transfiguration

MARIE: *With a short, self-satisfied sigh,* MARIE *crosses downstage left
and puts on a buckskin yoke and a pair of moccasins;
pennywhistle music begins.*

So many moccasins! *(short sigh, lifts pucksuck to her back, held
in place by a tumpline across her forehead; dragging canoe onto
stage)*

1 pair of moccasins per day per man
divided by 4 women
times 15 men on a one year expedition
equals 5,475 pairs of moccasins per year.

Lifts canoe overhead as if to portage.

So many moccasins!

Portaging in a counter-clockwise circle.

Une paire de moccassins par jour par homme,
divisé entre quatre femmes, ça fait également... so many
moccasins! C'est a dire, 5,475 pairs of moccasins per year.

*Sets canoe down, begins to unpack moccasins for repair,
downstage centre; to audience.*

Among my sisters I am the best moccasin maker. I have
three sisters, one older and two younger– but I'm the best
moccasin maker. That's why I am here. They came,
mistegoosoowuk, they came and told my father they had
no one to help them.

They had no one to make moccassins, to cook for them to
show them where to pick berries, to make canoes... no one
to help them. No one to help them.

Among my sisters I am the best moccasin maker, so my
father sent me. *(sits, unwraps moccasins)*

I'm not the only woman here. There are three other
women.

We women,
make moccasins/string snowshoes/teach them to
walk in the snow/make canoes.
We,
hunt/fish/put food away for the winter/teach them to
survive.
We,

in voice of CONTEMPORARY WOMAN #1:

translate/navigate/build alliances with our bodies/
loyalties through our blood.

in voice of MARIE:

We birth the Métis.

The Frenchman who is my husband, he has a big mustache
and eyes that I can look right through.

He calls himself Pierre and he calls me Marie. *(laughs)* My
name is Atchagoos Isquee' oo.

The Frenchman who is my husband he smokes a long pipe
of white clay, and in the evenings sometimes he sings:

"Marlbrough s'en va-t-en guerre
mi ron-ton, mi ron-ton mi montaine
Marlbrough
s'en va-t-en guerre
(ne) sais pas quand reviendra."

The Frenchman who is my husband, I sew him good
moccasins.

The moccasins I sew him, the stitches don't loosen at the
end of the day. The moccasins I sew him keep his big feet
dry and warm.

In the summer months we pick berries, we dry meat
so we can make pemmigan.

We women carry, *(packing up)*
tents/pots/tools/des couteaux/des fusiles/
hides for mocassins.

We carry,
cloth/beads/des miroirs/des épingles/des aîguilles
for the other people that we meet and we trade them for
their pelts;
Amisk/nigik/wachusk/sagweesoo/ateek/moosa.
Beaver/otter/muskrat/marten/mink/moose.
I speak for them when they have no words.

We portage with the canoes on our backs, (*picks up packsack
and canoe, continues circle*)

we portage, we portage.

We birth the Métis.

Une paire de moccassins par jour par homme,
divisé entre quatre femmes.

Among my sisters I'm the best moccasin maker.

MARIE *puts down canoe and packsack, notices* MARGARET'S
*calico dress hanging on post/ladder dowstage left along with her
kerchief and* MADELAINE'S *tartan shawl, she backs up, then
reaches for it; as the articles of clothing are removed from the
post, the mask faces of the hordes of Métis women are revealed.*

MUSICIAN: *Joined by* MARGARET *moans, interrupted by ratchet and
percussion instruments.*

MARGARET: *Putting on calico apron-dress, she is stunned, numb, rum-dumb.*
My husband didn't have a good hunt this season.

Putting on kerchief, ratchet sounds.

I am the third and youngest wife of a captain of the home
guard.
My husband didn't have a good hunt this season.

Ratchet sounds.

My husband likes the cloth, the blankets
that come from the Company trading post.
My husband doesn't wear skins and robes to keep him
warm.
My husband likes the liquor, the brandy, the whiskey
that come from the Company trading post.
My husband didn't have a good hunt this season.

Ratchet and rattle, turning walks upstage centre.

We didn't have many pelts to cure to scrape to stretch.
Not many beaver – only one moose...
even the rabbits were scarce.
We have no meat.
None to bring to the fort.
None for us to eat; not even for the children.
I am the third and youngest wife of a captain of the home
guard.
I have no children of my own. I help care for the children of
the other wives.
My husband didn't have a good hunt this season, so he
brought me into the fort; and he left with flour, sugar and
brandy.

Loud ratchet and percussive sounds; walking downstage centre.

The women, not from my people, but from the other side of
the river, they unbraid my hair and wash it
with harsh, lye soap. They wash me.
They can't leave any bear grease that protects my
skin from the winter and in the summertime from
the sun.
They say the company men will not like the way I
smell. *(Huge, tearing moan; as if being skinned alive.)*
They take away my deerskin clothes except for my
moccasins. They put on me clothing made of cloth
with little flowers.They twist my hair at the nape
of my neck. *(moaning; trying to speak,* MUSICIAN *joins)*
Mm... mm...mmy name is Wapithee'oo! They call me
Margaret. *(walking downstage centre to lip of stage)*
So, we scrub the forts and warm their beds... and
their beds...and their beds...
We quickly learn to love their alcohol:

Stumbles onto ramp.

the strong smell goes up my nose,
and burns my lips and tongue, it heats my throat.
I feel it travel to my stomach. It warms me from the
inside out.

Singing; very drunk.

"Ha, ha, ha you and me
little brown jug
don't I love thee?"
It makes me happy. It makes me laugh.
Iminigweeskeetchik! *(laughing)*
And after all it numbs the cold, it blurs their ugly,
square houses in the fort. *(stops laughing)* It numbs not
recognizing
the face of one company man from the next.

Lots of manic sound.

We die from
smallpox, syphilis, tuberculosis, childbirth.
We claw at the gate of the fort or we starve and
freeze to death outside.
We birth the Métis.
When there is no more to trade, our men trade us.
Fathers, uncles, brothers, husbands,trade us for
knives, axes, muskets liquor.
My husband didn't have a good hunt this season.

Chimes, moan, and ratchet; removes kerchief, adopts
MADELAINE'S *haughty stance.*

MADELAINE: YES! Yes, I did try to poison the new Mrs. Johnston!
Two days confined to her quarters with a stomach ache.

Puts on tartan shawl with cameo.

And I would do it again! Hang me, hang me then, I kill her
in my dreams. *(sits, downstage right)*
I am – I was married to James Johnston for fifteen years.
He easily won my father's favour - my father the chief
Factor, hmmn...? James was a suitable match.
My cameo – I still wear it pinned at my throat.
Two days! They left me only two days to get out.
Fifteen years null and void! Null and void in two days!

It is called "turning off".

"Turned off," he said, *(stands, crosses downstage centre)* "The
only way to tell you, Madelaine, is that you have been

turned off. But James has always been more than generous with you, Madelaine. But Madelaine, the arrangement has already been made."

Already been made?

"All your belongings can accompany you. There is a house, Madelaine, where you can live with Mr. Campbell, who has been very kind in accepting your husband's offer."

What reason? What reason? WHAT REASON?
... a white wife/a British woman...
... a white woman/a British wife.

Fifteen years, James Johnston.
In the morning they arrive and I can see her. Pale, weighted down with mountains and mountains of petticoats.
Trailing 14 trunks and a piano! She flounces into my house with my husband! *(strides up ramp downstage right)*

You only get my leavings! *(chimes)* I'll slit you open right through the belly, just like I skin a rabbit!
Ee goo speek ga aee tuk see gwow moonias swee wuk!

Stepping out of MADELAINE *downstage right, voice of* CONTEMPORARY WOMAN #1.

CONTEMPORARY WOMAN #1:
Which means, "When the White women came."
When Madelaine got angry, she would speak Cree, her mother's language.
So, when the White women came, "Les filles du roi", these women, who were the wives and daughters and granddaughters of the founders of this country –
were no longer women. And though turning off is no longer practiced, it is still an essential fiber in the fabric of our contemporary lives.

(back into MADELAINE'S *voice and time frame)*

MADELAINE: Saaa!! *(skinning motion)*
My china tea service came directly from England.

(begins to circle counter-clockwise and moving upstage centre)

All that way and not one broken! It's a full set;
with gold leaf around the rim of each cup.

(sits upstage centre)

I sit in my grandmother's old rocking chair...
My grandmother made moccasins in this chair and she
showed me how.
"You're a good girl with your hands Madelaine. Oui ma
fille, ça-y-est"
Now my hands don't move. They lie in my lap like two
dead birds, broken at the neck and lifeless.

(on tape):

Disposed of, discarded, replaced, after the white women
came.
Ee goo speek ga gee tuk see gwow moonias swee wuk.

MUSICIAN: *Singing with guitar while* CONTEMPORARY WOMAN #1 *sheds
shawl, kerchief, and calico dress and hangs them on the tree. The
buckskin yoke remains on.*

In the middle of my dream I came face to face to face
and the copper hand reached to touch my back.
I awakened sad, cold, confused, for the journey had been
long and far... avec Marie, Margaret et Madelaine...
avec Marie, Margaret et Madelaine... avec Marie, Margaret
et Madelaine, Madelaine... avec Marie Margaret et
Madelaine.

CONTEMPORARY WOMAN #2:
        Princess, Princess!

CONTEMPORARY WOMAN #1:
        Princess, Princess!

Transformation 10
Cigar Store Squaw/"You Light Up My Life"

PRINCESS BUTTERED-ON-BOTH-SIDES *as the* CIGAR STORE SQUAW
crosses to centrestage with an over-sized bunch of cigars.

PRINCESS BUTTERED-ON-BOTH-SIDES:

> *(offering cigars to audience)* UGH! I used to have this job,
> standing out in front of the tobacco store, but I didn't like
> the crowd. Besides, do you think anyone would talk to me?
> Not even chit chat. Do you think anyone would bring me a
> dozen roses, or an orchid corsage? No. Do you know what
> they gave me? Cigars. Do you know, the other day,
> somebody actually lit a match on me. Do you want to
> know where? *(indicates pelvic area)* So humiliating. But I
> want it all! I wanna be free to express myself! *(sets cigars
> down at tree)* I wanna be the girl next door! *(removes
> buckskin yoke in exasperation)* I wanna have lots and lots of
> blonde hair-great big blonde hair. I wanna be – Doris Day,
> Farrah Fawcett, Daryl Hannah – Oh,you know the one –
> Christie Brinkley! *(hums "Uptown Girl" while putting on
> white buckskin mini-dress)* I wanna be a cover girl, a beauty
> queen, Miss America, Miss North American Indian! That's
> it! According to the "Walk In Beauty Seminar" it's very,
> very important to have the right look. *(notices dress; screams
> in horror)* O.K. for the talent segment, but for the evening
> gown competion? The Finals? It's a rag! A rag! *(Reaches into
> pouch of buckskin dress, pulls out and reveals a shimmering
> evening gown of the tackiest sort, and velcroes it onto dress.)*

> Ahhh! Isn't this a devastating gown? I designed it myself.
> So, here I am a finalist in the Miss North American Indian
> Beauty Pageant! Think of it! Little me from in front of the
> tobacco store, fighting for DEMOCRACY!

> HELLO WORLD!!

HOST: *Enters upstage left with tablita-style corn "crown" and ear of corn "bouquet."*

And now, the moment you've all been waiting for... the winner of the 498th annual Miss North American Indian Beauty Pageant, from her woodland paradise... Miss Congeniality...

PRINCESS BUTTERED-ON-BOTH-SIDES!!!!

PRINCESS BUTTERED-ON-BOTH-SIDES:

Screaming; jumping up and down flat footed as Host presents her with her "bouquet" and "crowns" her with a headdress covered with small ears of corn which light up. She begins her triumphant walk down the runway, weeping and blowing kisses, while HOST *throws popcorn at her feet singing "You Light Up My Life", in true lounge lizard tradition. When* PRINCESS BUTTERED-ON-BOTH-SIDES *reaches upstage centre she strikes the pose of the Statue of Liberty, and the ears of corn on her headdress are illuminated in full. The following lines are spoken throughout her runway march:*

Thank-you, thank-you... Oh! I can't believe it! I love you all...

You have made my heart soar like a rabbit... I'll never forget this moment!

She unplugs herself; corn lights out. Exits upstage left. HOST *winds up cord from headdress, humming bars from "You Light Up My Life," removes jacket, bunches it up in front of her thighs as if it were a skirt; squats; prepares to sit as if on toilet; she continues to attempt to sit on toilet between each speech.*

Transformation 11

Las Ratas

CONTEMPORARY WOMAN #2:

It's really hard for me to go to a public washroom and when I do, it has to be fast, because if I stay long enough, this hand is going to come out of the water and grab me. Probably pull me in.

CONTEMPORARY WOMAN #1:

I never really knew Annie Mae. Though we'd been in the same place at the same time, we never really spoke.

CONTEMPORARY WOMAN #2:

"There is a rat in the toilet!" my father shouted. And there it was, dead, floating in the water. It's really hard for me to go to a public washroom.

CONTEMPORARY WOMAN #1:

My most vivid memory of her was when we came across each other at the Sundance. She was sitting leaning against a tree. We looked at each other and smiled, acknowledging the dust, the glaring heat, the desperate little breeze under the tree where we sat. The weight of our history on our backs, the tiredness of the struggle we shared.

CONTEMPORARY WOMAN #2:

After the coup, I read a testimonio of a 13 year old girl. She had been tortured. They were looking for her brother.

CONTEMPORARY WOMAN #1:

I never really knew Annie Mae, so when I heard about Annie Mae, murdered at the bottom of a cliff, reign of terror they called it – Annie Mae, beaten, raped, shot in the back of the head.

CONTEMPORARY WOMAN #2:

It's really hard for me to go to a public washroom.

CONTEMPORARY WOMAN #1:

When I think about Annie Mae, I think about her searching for her hands — the FBI lost her hands.

CONTEMPORARY WOMAN #2:

They interrogated her by inserting a live rat into her vagina. The tail of the rat was attached to a wire that was connected to the whole electrical system. With every question there would be an electric shock. It's really hard for me to go to a public washroom.

CONTEMPORARY WOMAN #1:

When I think about Annie Mae, I see her, a small woman, smiling against a tree. But her hands...

CONTEMPORARY WOMAN #2:

Now when I read this I was still a virgin and I didn't have the idea of what size something had to be in order to fit inside a vagina. Especially something as uncomfortable as a rat.

CONTEMPORARY WOMAN #1:

Her hands...

CONTEMPORARY WOMAN #2:

And the rats are really big in Chile.

Transformation 12

Contemporary Woman/Spirit/Animal Spirit

MUSICIAN: *(singing)*

And when the thunder strikes you in the
    heart of things,
You will remenber thoughts you never
    had before.
When the thunder strikes you in the heart.
    The thunder... the thunder ... the thunder....
        La la la la la la

Singing continues under following action until CONTEMPORARY
WOMAN#1 *speaks; she descends pyramid,* SPIRIT-SISTER *hands
her the pot of red paint which she offers to sky while walking to
centreslage, sinking to knees; in four gestures, she paints palms,
inner arms, neck, throat in reverence to the initiation and full
acceptance of mature womanhood; turning upslage left she offers
paint to pyramid; embraces tree upstage right, overwhelmed with
awe, moves downstage right.* SPIRIT-SISTER *guides and directs the
action in the following sequence which takes place in parallel
worlds of time and space.*

CONTEMPORARY WOMAN #1:

Stand me in the rain forest –
my soul whispers, "home...
home..." Rise me above the rain forest–

I know every ray of filtered
light that ripples the living
    green
*(falls; scrambles up ladder
downstage left)*
slant-eyed and head swinging
low to the ground,
my muscles ripple from
    shoulder to haunch,
now running – now stopping
    to sniff the air...

Voice of CONTEMP.
WOMAN #1: (*on
tape; singing*):
Cuando canto en Tulum, en
Tulum canta la luna–
cuando canto en Tulum, en
Tulum canta la luna.

(tape; singing)
When you tasted of salt
    and oranges,
and the moon sang her
    happiest songs to us,
– heart offerings
when we remembered
    her –
When you tasted of salt
    and oranges,
and the falling stars
    took our breath away,
– the waves of the sea
mixed with my own
    salt tears

(hanging from top rung; climbing down)

barefoot and possessionless I
walk resigned, but not broken,
chest thrust forward I memorize
every leaf, every hill, every
bird, every plot of mountain corn –
knowing these are
   the last things I will see.
The bus winds the mountain
   turns. It begins to rain,
     cold drops pelting the window
      in streaks.

(falls downstage centre)

SPIRIT-SISTER:
I promise to return.
The light in the
   doorways,
the hammocks hung in
   the homes
of the brown
mountain-weathered
     people looking up
from the side
   of the road.

CONTEMPORARY WOMAN #1:
   I promise to return
     to carry on
      the light.

(rising)

Swell my heart in my chest
   full and warm. I turn and
   say, "If I survive this
   journey, it is only because
   my heart has decided not to
     burst."

SPIRIT-SISTER:
...and she sounds like this:

(both singing)
ah ah ah   ah ah ah
        ah ah ah
        ah   ah   ah!

While singing, CONTEMPORARY WOMAN #1 *takes bucket of sand from base of tree; empties it centrestage; makes footprints.*

CONTEMPORARY WOMAN #1:

I give myself to this land.

Falls; hangs head and shoulders upsidedown off the lip of the stage.

My heart pierced, my back
    split open. Impaled.
My blood stains this piece
    of earth - a landmark
        for my soul.
I promise to return to
    love you always.   SPIRIT-SISTER:
                                        Call to me in a language
                                        I don't understand,

CONTEMPORARY WOMAN #1:

Rolls downstage right, comes to kneeling.

Curled beside me, you sleep.
Wake up! There's work to be done!
    We're here.

                                        SPIRIT-SISTER:
                                        slant-eyed and head
                                            swinging
                                            low to the ground,
                                            my spine arches from
                                                neck to tail.

CONTEMPORARY WOMAN #1:   *(tape; singing)*
                                        When you tasted of salt
                                            and oranges
(downstage centre, ramp)   I howled at the pulling
I crouch at the side   in my womb,
    of the mountain   – your own shaking
    the guardian–watching   not quieted by whispers–
                                            (of no, no, no)

When you tasted of salt
and oranges,

(add live voice; Contemporary Woman #1)
I put down my sorrow in
an ancient
place,
ahh ahh ahh ahh

(tape only)
wordless, I walk into
the sea

CONTEMPORARY WOMAN #1:
I wait.

and the moon she will sing.

(add live voices; Contemporary Woman #1 *and* Spirit-Sister)
ah ah ah   ah ah ah
ah ah ah
AH   AH   AH!

Transformation 13

Una Nacion

Lights snap to bright – sudden transition to mundane, urban environment.

CONTEMPORARY WOMAN #1:
(standing on ramp stage left) It's International Women's Day–

No, I didn't go to the march. *(cross to centrestage, very deliberately making footprints in sand)* So many years of trying to fit into feminist shoes. O.K., I'm trying on the shoes; but they're not the same as the shoes in the display case. The shoes I'm trying on must be crafted to fit these wide, square, brown feet. I must be able to feel the earth through their soles.

So, it's International Women's Day, and here I am. Now, I'd like you to take a good look – *(turns slowly, all the way around)* I don't want to be mistaken for a crowd of Native women. I am one. And I do not represent all Native women. I am one.

Crosses to tree upstage right; brings empty basin and pitcher of water centrestage.

And since it can get kind of lonely here, I've brought some friends, sisters, guerrilleras – the women – "Word Warriors," to help.

Pours water into basin; CONTEMPORARY WOMAN #2 *approaches, kneels by basin, they wet each other's faces, hair, and arms; purifying. With a cupped handful of water each, they sprinkle stage in opposite circles.*

CONTEMPORARY WOMAN #1:
    (in front of pyramid, upstage left) Gloria Anzaldúa!

CONTEMPORARY WOMAN #2:
    (singing softly, under throughout)
    Una nación no sera conquistada...
    hasta que los corazones de sus mujeres
    caigan a la tierra.

CONTEMPORARY WOMAN #1:
    "What I want is the freedom to carve and chisel my own face, to staunch the bleeding with ashes, to fashion my own gods out of my entrails."

Dips hand in basin again, sprinkles water to stage right.

Diane Burns describes that to hold a brown-skinned lover means: *(face to face, they wash each other's chests over heart)* "...we embrace and rub the wounds together."
She also says: "This ain't no stoic look, this is my face."

Dips hand in basin again, sprinkles half circle.

The Kayapo woman, of the Rain Forest, who stands painted, bare to the waist, holding a baby by the hand, and confronts the riot squad in the capital of Brazil *(walks downstage centre)* and says: *(gesturing with arm; punctuating)* "I am here to speak for my brother and my brother-in-law.

Where are your sisters to cry out for you? I am enraged with you! You steal our land! I am calling upon you! I throw my words in your faces!!!!"

Drum kicks in loudly, a "call to arms"; song begins in Spanish to an Andean rhythm and evolves into a round dance – a "49" – contemporary Native song with English words.

CONTEMPORARY WOMAN #2:

(singing; full out)
Una nación no sera conquistada hasta que los corazones
de sus mujeres caigan a la tierra.

CONTEMPORARY WOMAN #1:

(joins)
Una nación no sera conquistada hasta que los corazones
de sus mujeres caigan a la tierra.
No importa que los guerreros sean valientes o que sus armas
sean poderosas!

During the following musical transition, sung once through without English words, the drum's rhythm changes to the heartbeat of the round dance.

CONTEMPORARY WOMAN #1:

A nation is not conquered until the hearts of its women
are on the ground.

CONTEMPORARY WOMAN #2:

(joins)
Then, it is done, no matter how brave
its warriors, nor how strong its weapons.

Blind Faith leaps in the dark

BLACKOUT

Bibliography

RECOMMENDED

Poetry, Narratives, Testimonies:

A Gathering of Spirit; Beth Brant, ed.; Firebrand Books and Women's Press, 1984, 1988.

Borderlands/La Frontera; Gloria Anzaldúa; Spinsters/Aunt Lute Book Company, 1987.

Loving in the War Years; Cherríe Moraga; South End Press, 1983.

Not Vanishing; Chrystos; Press Gang, 1988.

Riding the One-Eyed Ford; Diane Burns; Contact II Publications, 1981.

The Sacred Hoop; Paula Gunn Allen; Beacon Press, 1986.

This Bridge Called My Back: Writings by Radical Women of Color; Cherríe Moraga and Gloria Anzaldúa, eds.; Kitchen Table: Women of Color Press, 1981, 1983.

Biography and History:

Many Tender Ties: Women in Fur-Trade Society in Western Canada 1670-1870; Sylvia Van Kirk; Watson and Dwyer, 1980.

Moon, Sun, And Witches: Gender Ideologies and Class in Inca and Colonial Peru; Irene Silverblatt; Princeton University Press, 1987.

Pocahontas and Her World; Phillip L. Barbour; Houghton Mifflin, 1970.

Symbols of the United States: From Indian Queen to Uncle Sam, E. McClung Fleming in *The Frontiers of American Culture*; Ray B. Browne et al., ed., Lafayette, Indiana; Perdue University Press, 1967, pp. 1-24

The Mother of Us All: Pocahontas Reconsidered; Phillip Young; Kenyon Review 24 (Summer 1962) pp. 391-441.

The Pocahontas Perplex: the Image of Indian Women in American Culture Retrospect and Prospect; Rayna Green; first published in *Mass. Review* #16, Autumn 1975, pp. 698-714. Reprinted in *Unequal Sisters: A Multi-Cultural Reader in U.S. Women's History*, Eds. Ellen DuBois and Vicki Ruiz. New York: Rutledge, Kegan & Paul, 1990.

NOT RECOMMENDED (but useful from the dominant culture perspective)

Fire and Blood: a History of Mexico; T.R. Fehrenbach; Collier, 1980.

Pocahontas; Ingri and Edgar Parin d'Aulaire; Doubleday, 1946.

Pocahontas, Girl of Jamestown; Kate Jassen; Troll Associates, 1979.

The Double Life of Pocahontas; Jean Fritz; Putnam, 1983.

The Pathfinder: the Newsletter of the American Indian Heritage Foundation; (sponsors of the Miss Indian America Pageant, Princess Pale Moon).

Birdwoman and the Suffragettes:
a Story of Sacajawea

A Play for Radio

Dedicated to Sacajawea, 1786-1884
whoever she may have been; and to
all the unnamed women who share her story.

Production Notes

BIRD WOMAN AND THE SUFFRAGETTES: a Story of Sacajawea
was first produced in 1991 for CBC Radio Drama's *Vanishing Point –
Adventure Stories for Big Girls.*

PRODUCTION:

Executive Producer:	Bill Lane
Producer:	Banuta Rubess
Technician:	Joanne Arka
Sound:	John Stewart
Production Assistant:	Nina Callaghan
Script Editor:	Ann Jansen
Music Composition:	Jani Lauzon, Steve Hunter
Musicians:	Jani Lauzon, Steve Hunter, Don Francks

CAST:

Sacajawea	Monique Mojica
Suffragette #1, Granny #1	Jani Lauzon
Suffragette #2, Granny #3	Gloria Miguel
Suffragette #3	Patricia Idlette
Granny #2	Juanita Rennie
Captain Meriweather Lewis, York	Marc Gomes
Captain William Clark	Henry Czerny
Grandpa #1, Charbonneau	Denis LaCroix
Grandpa #2	Jim Mason
Indian Boy	Jason Martin

SCENE 1: Street: A Gathering of Suffragettes

Suffragette's Theme Song/March

*Sounds like a kid's T.V. show; Mr. Rogers, or Howdy
Doody with heavy flavor of Gilbert and Sullivan and the
sound of marching feet.*

SUFFRAGETTES:

(sung)	Far away o'er the mountains lived a brave Indian maid– so that her name n'ere be forgotten, and her mem'ry never fade:
(spoken)	Now remember:
(sung)	there's Sacajawea Creek in Montana Sacajawea Lake In Washington Sacajawea Lake in North Dakota and Sacajawea Springs in Idaho
(spoken)	And that's not all,
(sung)	there's Sacajawea Peak in Montana Sacajawea Peak in Wyoming Sacajawea Peak, Wallowa Range, Oregon and Sacajawea Peak in Idaho
(spoken)	...and Pompcy's Pillar for "Little Pomp"

SCENE 2: Big Tent

Murmurings of the crowd

SUFFRAGETTE #3: Good evening, sister suffragettes. I am proud to present the chairman of the Oregon Equal Suffrage Association, Eva Emery Dye.

SUFFRAGETTE #1: Sacajawea, as we all know was the trusty little Indian guide who led the first white men over the Rocky Mountains and to the Pacific shore. Thus, her faithful servitude resulted in the successful completion of the famous expedition of Captains Meriweather Lewis and William Clark, whose "Corps of Discovery" was commissioned by President Thomas Jefferson to explore the immense territory west of the Missouri river and make it property of the United States. It is with great pride that I announce that Portland is planning a monument in honour of Sacajawea for the 1905 Lewis and Clark Exposition!

(applause from crowd)

In order to ensure that the identity of Sacajawea is known to you and above all, that veracity itself is upheld, I will now read from my historical novel, "The Conquest: The True Story Of Lewis and Clark."

"Sacajawea, modest princess of the Shoshones, heroine of the great expedition, stood with her babe in arms and smiled upon them from the shore. So had she stood in the Rocky Mountains pointing out the gates. So had she followed the great rivers, navigating the continent. Sacajawea's hair was neatly braided, her nose was fine and straight, and her skin pure copper like a statue in some Florentine gallery. Madonna of her race, she had led the way to a new time. To the hands of this girl, not yet eighteen, had been entrusted the key that unlocked the road to Asia.

Someday, upon the Bozeman Pass, Sacajawea's statue will stand beside that of Clark. Someday, where the rivers part, her laurels will vie with those of Lewis. Across North America, a Shoshone princess touched hands with Jefferson, opening her country."

(applause from crowd)

I will now issue an appeal to women's organizations across the country to defray the cost of commissioning this statue. The sculptor commisioned for this occasion is Alice Cooper of Denver, Colorado.

We need to raise $7,000.00! We must all do our part! We will sell Sacajawea buttons and Sacajawea spoons...!

(the crowd roars; faint refrain of Suffragette's Theme turns into Sacajawea soundscape)

SCENE 3: The Plains

Wind, swishing grass.

SACAJAWEA: It was before Tsakakawea became my name
        they called me...
Pohenaif... Pohenaif, from where the tall grass dances
        laughs and ripples
where the sky meets the earth
        the grass dances to the east of me
        whispers mysteries to the north of me
        sighs its sorrow to the west of me
        and sings again in the south.
Pohenaif... Pohenaif, from where the
        tall grass always moving greets the
          sun at dawn.
I am Pohenaif
        I am Grass Woman.
So it was before Tsakakawea became my
        name that the
        Mandan came upon us at the river -
Captured! Slave girl,
        hush, keep quiet!
        no tears for the slave girl
        earth houses, skin boats
        slave girl of the Mandan.
Mother! – Silence
        but for the little ones
        crying in the night.
My footprints no longer leave
        the mark of the Shoshone
        my mocassins are Mandan.
Slave girl plants
        seeds in the earth
        and longs for where the mountains
        rise to pierce the Sky World
        and the hunger spirits wait.

(music out)

SCENE 4 : Campfire: Grannies' tea party
Wind River Shoshone Reservation, 1926

Fire crackling, wind blowing in grasses, dog barking.

GRANNY #1: (*groans as she lowers herself to sit, sighs*)
Hmmnn... so much commotion in the house, early this morning another great-great grandchild they brought me to name – girl this time.

ALL GRANNIES: Hmn.., eh heh, oh yes...(etc.)

GRANNY #1: They were arguing – they wanted to name her Sacajawea – Birdwoman. What do you think of that?

GRANNY #3: That tea ready, yet?

Tea being ladled from pot.

GRANNY #2: (*drinking noisily*) Good and hot. Any sugar?

I knew Porivo or Sacajawea, at Fort Bridger. She lived with her son, Bazil. I was a young girl at that time, maybe at the age of 14 or 15.

GRANNY #3: You know, she was always looked upon by the women of the band as the leader.

ALL GRANNIES: (*agreeing*) Hmn... eh heh, oh yes... (etc.)

GRANNY #2: "Porivo or Chief Woman, whom the whites call Sacajawea was well-known among us and I especially knew her very well. She spoke French as well as her sons.

I remember when she was very old and living on this reservation, she told about feeding some hungry white men with dog meat..."

GRANNY #1: (*interrupting*) Yes! "I remember that Sacajawea told my mother that while she was travelling with a large body of people when army officers were in charge, the people became very hungry."

GRANNY #3: (*overlapping*) "I remember her once telling that she had fed the whites with dog meat." Why don't they put that in their statues and big pictures of her?

ALL GRANNIES: (*giggle*)

GRANNY #2:   "She spoke five different languages: Shoshone, Comanche, Gros Ventre, Assiniboine and French."

GRANNY #3:   "She said that she had married a Frenchman and that she had travelled with some white men toward the setting sun... she told many times of her wanderings, I cannot clearly remember all of them."

Lewis and Clark theme swells up.

SCENE 5: Living Room
Lewis and Clark – Mandan Territory, November, 1804.

Music out; grandfather clock, papers rustling.

CLARK: (*clears his throat*) Hail Redskins! I bring greetings from the Great White Father in Washington – No, no... Washington... Redskins... um... no. Hello Savages! You may now discard the flags of France and Spain and accept these medals bearing the likeness of the Great White Father in Washington. See how they shine!

Door opens; footsteps.

LEWIS: Oh, Clark, packing I see, carry on...and don't forget, William, a good quantity of tobacco twists should prove very useful in trading with the Indians.

CLARK: Yes, Lewis, certainly. We have already several boxes of Indian gifts which include: fancy coats, Jefferson Medals, flags, knives, tomahawks, looking glasses, handkerchiefs, paints, beads and other assorted ornaments.

LEWIS: Very good. Care for a pipeful?

CLARK: Wouldn't mind.

Striking of match.

LEWIS: (*sucking pipe*) Clark?

CLARK: (*sucking pipe*) Yes Lewis?

LEWIS:	What do you think of this Charbonneau who appeared in camp today offering his services as interpreter?
CLARK:	Ah, Toussaint Charbonneau, the Canuck. Seemed rather a lout to me. And the Indians don't like him much, that is if you can judge by the names that they've given him: Chief of the Little Village, Great Horse from Abroad, Squaw Man and Man-Part Never Limp.
BOTH:	*Chuckle.*
LEWIS:	Nevertheless, he is well known as a trapper, and he does speak Minnataree.
CLARK:	*(under breath)* Well known for raping Indian girls...
LEWIS:	What?
CLARK:	Well, if you must know, I don't like him.
LEWIS:	Nor do I; but consider this: our other interpreter, Jussome, speaks Mandan, and Charbonneau, Minnetaree, but it is the Shoshone we must parlee with in order to procure horses at the crucial point when we must traverse the Rocky Mountains. *(shrewdly)* Why hire yet another interpreter when Charbonneau has three Snake wives of the Shoshone, am I correct?
CLARK:	Good God! You're not proposing that we bring three women with us?
LEWIS:	No, of course not. Only one. The bright-eyed one, I think, with the red-painted part in her hair.
CLARK:	But she is big with child!!
LEWIS:	Yes, but so big, in fact, that she is sure to give birth before we continue. I don't foresee her being any trouble. They're not like our women, you know; if she had enough to eat and a few trinkets to wear I believe she would be content anywhere.
CLARK:	I do see your point; and seeing as the squaw is a wife of Charbonneau, she won't be expecting to be paid.

LEWIS: Settled then? Charbonneau it is.

CLARK: *(sighs)* Settled. But I still don't like him.

                  Sacajawea theme comes in strong.

SCENE 6

River: The storm – June 29, 1805

Rapidly moving river, men paddling canoes, shouts over.

SACAJAWEA (INT.): These boats – not round, nor made
                   of skin like the Mandan's
                   but long, made of wood with a
                   large sail flapping like a
                   single wing.
                   Many days now we have travelled on the river.
                       They call my baby Little Pomp–
                       his name is Jean Baptiste
                   he looks into my face and blinks - his shining eyes
                       black as stones.
                   I see his father ahead of me -
                       Charbonneau – I am his woman
                       won gambling – because he likes
                       his Indian wives very young
                       His beard stings like nettles on my skin.

*Hawk's whistle, wind rustling through leaves, storm
begins, under.*

SACAJAWEA (INT.): They call me Tsakakawea – Birdwoman!
                       I fly high above the river
                       hover and glide - watch the boat
                       no sound but leaves as wind
                   ruffles their light underside – rain coming...

CLARK: *(in distance)* Rain coming!

SACAJAWEA (INT.): Rain coming! a shout, my beak frozen
                       as the sky turns black, purple, yellow, grey.
                       No sound – then the river roars angry
                       spitting white foam, rising, rising,

>The storm opens wide its mouth to
>>suck us under!
>Tsakakawea – Birdwoman, wings spread
>>diving for the boat!

Hawk's screech, heavy winds, rapids.

CLARK: *(in distance)* Quick! Get us to shore! Lively now!
Charbonneau!

Move, man! Charbonneau, to the shore!

SACAJAWEA (INT.): Red Hair Captain Clark sweats –
Charbonneau cannot swim
>a shelf of rock, safety from the river
>a wall of water tears rocks and mud – standing in a
>pool of rising mud water – I pull my son from
>>his cradle...his clothes are swallowed by the river.
Up the hill climbing – slipping in mud
>Charbonneau is frightened and cannot move.

CLARK: Janey! Hurry Janey! Blast it Charbonneau,
Give a hand here! Charbonneau!

SACAJAWEA (INT.): Red Hair Captain shouts, pushes me before him, Shouts!
>Charbonneau is frightened and has no strength
>I grab dead roots in the bank.

Shouting voices, feet running, panting, moving on, baby
crying under.

YORK: Captain Clark! Captain Clark! Janey! Is the child alright?

SACAJAWEA (INT.): My friend, Ben York, black whiteman runs along the
>bank
big chest heaving with his breath, and we are safe.
>I hold my screaming baby between my breasts
to warm him – and Charbonneau shivers like a dog.

SCENE 7: Street

Suffragette's theme song with marching feet.

Hand and hand with sister suffrage
   will she walk forever more –
through the vast and pathless mountains
   to the ocean's teeming shore.

(spoken)	And so...
(sung)	there's a Sacajawea plaque in Montana
	Sacajawea plaque in Wyoming
	Sacajawea plaque in North Dakota
and a	Sacajawea plaque in Idaho
(spoken)	in addition to.
(sung)	a Sacajawea statue in St. Louis
	Sacajawea statue in Virginia
	Sacajawea statue in Oklahoma
and a	Sacajawea statue in Idaho.
(spoken)	... and Pompey's Pillar for "Little Pomp."

SCENE 8: Parlour: Suffragette's tea party, 1905

Tea pouring, china clinking, happy sighs.

SUFFRAGETTE #2: ...so I said to her, 'What, no horseradish? A roast beef without horseradish simply is not a roast beef.'

SUFFRAGETTE #1: Ummn... I should say not. More tea dear?

Tea pouring.

SUFFRAGETTE #3: As I understand it, "the great difficulty was to cross the Rockies – to go from where the Missouri ended to where the Columbia began." Wilderness! All of it wilderness, wild and savage!

SUFFRAGETTE #2: Oh how exhilarating! Imagine! Oh how I've always wanted to be like a wild Indian – an Indian maiden dancing naked in the wilderness to the light of the bonfire!

SUFFRAGETTE #1: How lovely your daughter sang in church today, dear.

SUFFRAGETTE #2:	What? Oh... oh yes... thank-you.
SUFFRAGETTE #3:	So just how was it that you discovered this enchanting creature, Sa- ca- ca... um...Sa-ca-JAR-we-a?
SUFFRAGETTE #1:	Well, my dears, "I struggled along the best I could trying to find a heroine. I traced down every old book and scrap of paper, but was still without a real heroine. Finally I came upon the name of Sacajawea, and I screamed, 'I have found my heroine!'"
SUFFRAGETTE #3:	How marvellous for you, really!
SUFFRAGETTE #1:	Yes. "I then hunted up every fact I could find about Sacajawea. Out of a few dry bones I created Sacajawea and made her a living entity. For months I dug and scraped for accurate information about this wonderful Indian maid."
SUFFRAGETTE #2:	Imagine the excitement, the romance of trekking across the untamed, untouched, VIRGIN territory with those two handsome captains!! She must have been terribly in love with one of them... (I think it must have been Clark with that red hair.)
SUFFRAGETTE #3:	Well, the wheels of progess do turn. How fortunate for her people that the wilderness has been tamed and civilized – they're all Americans, now, and maybe we can teach them something about true equality.

SCENE 8: Campfire:
Grannies' tea party
Wind River Indian Reservation – 1926

Crackling fire, dogfight in distance, wind in the grasses.

GRANNY #2:	Put some more water on to boil, now, make sure there's plenty of tea in the pot.
GRANNY #1:	"The story of my grandmother is told in this way: We Comanche never knew that my grandmother had been married before she married my grandfather. We never knew that my grandmother had married a

	white man by the name of Charbonneau and guided some soldiers across the Rocky Mountains to the sea."
GRANNY #3:	"Baptiste, the son of Porivo, married two of my sisters."
GRANNY #1:	"She married Jerk Meat and had five children. My father was her second son. We heard she lived among the white people –"
GRANNY #3:	*(interrupts)* – "She was perfectly familiar with the white people at the fort. I mean that she was not afraid to mingle with them. The white people respected her."
GRANNY #2:	See, look here, these – women for suffering came and gave us these little spoons, eh? That woman on the spoon there, it's supposed to be Sacajawea. *(laughs)*
ALL GRANNIES:	*Giggle.*
	Clinking of stirring spoon under.
GRANNY #2:	Stirs tea just the same – when there's sugar. *(sighs)*
GRANNY #2:	"I remember very distinctly that she was very much interested in the treaty that Washakie was making with the whites at Fort Bridger, and I also remember that she was the only woman that spoke at the councils making the treaty. I was there and saw her speak."
GRANNY #1:	"We Comanches thought she had been killed until a Comanche boy named Howard met a Shoshone boy by the name of McAdams at that Carlisle Indian School. Then we found out that she was at Fort Washakie and died here."
GRANNIES:	*Exclamations of surprise.*
GRANNY #2:	Well, we Shoshones never thought too much of her taking those white men over the mountains to the big waters. It never was important to us. It made her important to the white people, though. So they gave her a medal and some papers to prove that she was worth something.
	What I have said is absolutely the truth. I am not trying to pretend at all. I am telling the truth.

SCENE 10: Street Scene:
St. Louis – 1806

Sacajawea theme with horses hooves on cobblestone;
bustling crowd under.

SACAJAWEA (INT.): St. Louis–
      open jaws on the shores
        of the river
  So many whites- busy as termites!
      Who do they see?
  I walk looking straight ahead
      my eyes bore a hole in
        Charbonneau's back.
  Baptiste in his cradleboard
        sings to himself.
      Who do they see in St. Louis?
  We stop and enter the home of
        Red hair Captain
  (exhalation of relief)
        and the door closes against
          the poison eyes.

Music out.

SCENE 11: Doorstep of House

Door opens; street in background.

CLARK: Ah, Charbonneau, and your femme, Sa-ca- ca ...
Janey! How anxious I have been to see my little
dancing boy, Baptiste. My boy Pomp!

Baby sounds, cooing, laughter.

SACAJAWEA (INT.): ... MY child, MY child.

Paper crackle.

CLARK: I see my letter has been safely delivered into your
hands, Charbonneau. I had my doubts that you
would come, seeing that you've insisted on going
back among the Indians.

CHARBONNEAU: *(more a growl than a word)* Oui.

SCENE 12: Livingroom

Door closes, footsteps on carpet, grandfather clock.

CLARK:
— But, what's this? You haven't even opened the letter — you can't read, can you? Very well, I'll read it to you:

Crackle of paper.

(*reading*) "Charbonneau, sir: Your present situation with the Indians gives me some concern – I wish now I had advised you to come on with me, where it most probably would be in my power to put you on some way to do something for yourself and for your little son, (my boy Pomp), you well know my fondness for him and my anxiety to take him and raise him as my own child."

CHARBONNEAU:
Oui.

Music returns.

SACAJAWEA (INT.):
Between my ribs a knife
   stabs – and I cannot speak!
     my heart drums:
     MY child, MY child
I hold him against my chest
     MY child, MY child
I brush my lips against
   his hair, the smallness of his head.
To hold him always so,
   that he never can be taken away!

CLARK:
"If you will bring your son to me, I will educate him and treat him as my own child."

CHARBONNEAU:
Oui.

CLARK:
Ah, Janey, I see you're still wearing the medal. Good girl. I know you deserved a greater reward for your services but in time it may prove very useful to you, to show that you are worth something...

SACAJAWEA (INT.):
...worth something?

CHARBONNEAU:
(*a growl*) Non. Trop petit.

SACAJAWEA (INT.):   Too small, he says.

Music rises and ends.

SCENE 13: Campfire:
Grandpas & Grannies
Wind River Indian Reservation, 1926

Crackling fire, laughing children run by, wind in grass.

GRANDPA #1:   Whenever she told that story of one of the "Big Soldiers" wanting to take Baptiste and educate him, "she would throw open her arms as if to surround him and hold him close. She would say: 'I wanted to hold my baby right here.'"

GRANDPA #2:   Hmnn, eh heh, that's so.

GRANNY #3:   Two more cups, sister, these men will have some tea.

Men groaning as they sit; match srtikes.

GRANDPA #1:   (*sucking on pipe*)... "and as to this medal, it must be remembered that Charbonneau wore it and then he died, then Sacajawea wore it and died, then Baptiste wore it and died, finally his brother Bazil wore it and died, and the Shoshone people declared it was no good, because everyone who wore it had died."

GRANNIES,
GRANDPA #2:   (*sounds of agreement*) Hmmn, eh-heh, that's so.

GRANNY #2:   I remember her son, Bazil, was buried with that medal. Someone said that on one side was the head of God.

GRANDPA #2:   "As near as I can remember, when I first saw my grandmother, Porivo, or Sacajawea,. She was still active, smart, and often took part in the councils." She was very much respected in spiritual ways,too. From her travels among the nations of the plains, "my grandmother introduced the sacred Sun Dance among this tribe and my father, Bazil, was made leader of that dance by my grandmother. I am today leader of that sacred ceremony because we did not have Sun Dance among the Shoshone before that."

GRANNY #3: Chief Washakie, respected Sacajawea very highly, above the ordinary Indian woman. She knew the ways of the whites so when it came time to make the treaty that made this reservation, Sacajawea stood and she spoke up for us here, to make sure things went right for us.

GRANDPA #1: She always spoke of the big waters, that is the water that goes on around the world.

Match strikes.

(*thoughtfully after a long exhale*) "Personally, I would like to ask, what is all of this fuss about?" We remember our grandmother for who she was to us –

ALL: *Sounds of agreement.*

GRANDPA #1: – not with medals, papers and monuments. "She is here on the hill in the cemetery. She can only be buried in one place."

GRANNY #1: Yes, yes that's true. I think I'll find another name for my new great-great-granddaughter. Let Sacajawea rest.

SCENE 14: Cavernous Hall:
The Statue Unveiled
Portland, Oregon – 1905

Faint, distorted refrain of Suffragette's theme, under; a large crowd of people in a cavernous hall.

SUFFRAGETTE #1: Ladies and Gentlemen, officials of the Lewis and Clark Centennial Exposition, it is my honor to present Susan B. Anthony.

SUSAN B. ANTHONY: "This is the first time in history that a statue has been erected in memory of a woman who accomplished patriotic deeds... This recognition of the assistance ren-

dered by a woman in the discovery of this great section
of the country is but the beginning of what is due..."

Applause fading under Sacajawea theme, cramped.

SACAJAWEA (INT.): *(hollow, encased)*
They call me Tsakakawea – Birdwoman
Porivo-Chief Woman
Shoshone Woman
But who are these strange sisters,
and what mountains are they climbing?
I feel the flag being pulled from
my bronze face
pulled from
my bronze arm pointing westward–
but I only wanted to go back home!
I see a small Indian boy,
as the flag floats
above my head
I hear him sing:

The Star-Spangled Banner.

INDIAN BOY: Oh say can you see
by the dawn's early light
What so proudly we hailed
at the twilight's last gleaming.
Whose broad stripes and bright stars

through the perilous night
O'er the ramparts we watched
were so gallantly streaming.
And the rockets red glare!
the bombs bursting in air!
Gave proof through the night
that our flag was still there
O say does the Star Spangled Banner
yet wave
O'er the land of the free ...
and the home of the brave.

SUFFRAGETTE #1: *(over)* Ladies and gentlemen, the President of the
National American Women's Suffrage Association:
Dr. Anna Howard Shaw!

SUFFRAGETTE #2: "We pay our tributes of honor and gratitude to the modest, unselfish, enduring little Shoshone squaw, who uncomplainingly trailed, canoed, climbed, slaved and starved with the men of the party, enduring all they endured... silently strapping her papoose upon her back she led the way, interpreting and making friendly overtures to powerful tribes of Indians, who but for her might at any moment have annihilated that brave band of intrepid souls... Forerunner of civilization, great leader of men, patient and motherly woman, we bow our hearts to do you honor!... May we the daughters of an alien race... learn the lessons of calm endurance in our efforts to lead men through the Pass of justice, which goes over the mountains of prejudice and conservatism to broad land of the perfect freedom of a true republic; one in which men and women together shall in perfect equality solve the problems of a nation that knows no caste, no race, no sex in opportunity, in responsibility or in justice! May 'the eternal womanly' ever lead us on!!"

Suffragette's theme — music only — sneaks in, under.

SACAJAWEA: *Breathing with difficulty.*

SACAJAWEA (INT.): Captured again!
Frozen! Cast in bronze,
    this hollow form with my name –
        Tsakakawea!
Who are these strange sisters?
and what mountains are they
    climbing?
"Brave," they say –
"Squaw," they say –
"Madonna," they say?
(laughing)
C'est a dire, comme la vierge, Marie?
    la vierge,
        married both to Charbonneau and
        Jerk Meat..
Who are these strange sisters?

If you remember me,
    remember a child fighting to stay alive
    remember a slave girl gambled away
    remember a mother protecting her child
    remember a wife defying the whip
    remember an old one who loved her people
    remember I died at home on my land.
Now, the Birdwoman's name –
    Tsakakawea
is caged in statues, paintings,
    lakes and rivers
      mountains, peaks and ridges
      poems made of fog and lies
and, ... and a flying machine
"The Spirit of Sacajawea" – Oh!
    (low laughter)
    cannot contain the spirit
so, high above the clouds,

Hawk's screech.

the Birdwoman beats her wings,
    sounds her voice,
    soars,
    and is free.

Suffragette's theme song returns full force.

SUFFRAGETTES: There's a silver service set now
    on the battleship Wyoming
      an intermezzo and a cantata
      bearing the name Sacajawea
(spoken)   So remember...
(sung)   there's a Sacajawea mural in Montana
            Sacajawea Park in Washington
            Sacajawea Camp in Wyoming
    and   Sacajawea Museum in Idaho.
(spoken)   and that's not all...

⊕   ⊕   ⊕

BIBLIOGRAPHY

RECOMMENDED
(with a historical grain of salt)

Sacajawea; Grace Raymond Hebard; A.H. Clark, 1957.

Sacajawea of the Lewis and Clark Expedition; Ella E. Clark and Margot Edwards; University of California Press, 1979.

NOT RECOMMENDED
(romanticized historical novels; good source material for satire)

Sacajawea; Anna Lee Waldo; Avon Books, 1978.

Sacajawea – Bird Woman; James Willard Schultz; Houghton Mifflin, 1918.

About the Playwright

Monique Mojica is a Kuna-Rappahannock half-breed, a woman word-warrior, a mother and an actor. Born in New York City, she came to Canada as a founding member of Native Earth Performing Arts and is a former Artistic Director of that company. As a Toronto-based stage, television and film actor, Monique has performed in numerous acclaimed productions including creating the role of Marie-Adele Starblanket in The Rez Sisters. She also played the title role in Theatre Passe Muraille's award-winning production of Jessica, and was seen as Ariel in Skylight Theatre's production of The Tempest. Princess Pocahontas and the Blue Spots, Monique's first full-length script, was co-produced by Nightwood Theatre and Theatre Passe Muraille and enjoyed a month's run at TPM in 1990.

Excerpts from Princess Pocahontas and the Blue Spots are included in three anthologies to be published in 1992: Canadian Native Anthology, Oxford Press, Indigenous Women's Writings: Canadian Plains, Crane Editions and Interplay: Sex, Gender and Voice in the Canadian Theatre, Simon and Pierre Publishers. Ms. Mojica has also written for TV Ontario's Many Voices anti-racism series, and has been commissioned by The Great Canadian Theatre Company as one of twelve playwrights to participate in a project entitled Stolen Lands: 1492-1992.

Monique is the guest editor for Canadian Theatre Review's special issue on Native theatre, Fall 1991 and Playwright in Residence for Nightwood Theatre in 1991-92.